Thanksgiving Day

By ALLAN MOREY

Illustrations by BRIAN HARTLEY

Music by ERIK KOSKINEN

CANTATA
LEARNING

WWW.CANTATALEARNING.COM

CANTATA
LEARNING

Published by Cantata Learning
1710 Roe Crest Drive
North Mankato, MN 56003
www.cantatalearning.com

Library of Congress Cataloging-in-Publication Data
Names: Morey, Allan, author. | Hartley, Brian, illustrator. | Koskinen, Erik,
  composer.
Title: Thanksgiving Day / by Allan Morey ; Illustrations by Brian Hartley ;
  music by Erik Koskinen.
Description: North Mankato, MN : Cantata Learning, [2018] | Includes
  bibliographical references and index.
Identifiers: LCCN 2017007523 (print) | LCCN 2017016303 (ebook) | ISBN
  9781684100569 | ISBN 9781684100552 (hardcover : alk. paper)
Subjects: LCSH: Thanksgiving Day--Juvenile literature. | Thanksgiving
  Day--Songs and music.
Classification: LCC GT4975 (ebook) | LCC GT4975 .M67 2018 (print) | DDC
  394.2649--dc23
LC record available at https://lccn.loc.gov/2017007523

978-1-68410-282-2 (paperback)

Book design, Tim Palin Creative
Editorial direction, Flat Sole Studio
Executive musical production and direction, Elizabeth Draper
Music arranged and produced by Erik Koskinen

Printed in the United States of America.
0390

ACCESS THE MUSIC!
SCAN CODE WITH MOBILE APP
CANTATALEARNING.COM

TIPS TO SUPPORT LITERACY AT HOME

WHY READING AND SINGING WITH YOUR CHILD IS SO IMPORTANT

Daily reading with your child leads to increased academic achievement. Music and songs, specifically rhyming songs, are a fun and easy way to build early literacy and language development. Music skills correlate significantly with both phonological awareness and reading development. Singing helps build vocabulary and speech development. And reading and appreciating music together is a wonderful way to strengthen your relationship.

READ AND SING EVERY DAY!

TIPS FOR USING CANTATA LEARNING BOOKS AND SONGS DURING YOUR DAILY STORY TIME

1. As you sing and read, point out the different words on the page that rhyme. Suggest other words that rhyme.

2. Memorize simple rhymes such as Itsy Bitsy Spider and sing them together. This encourages comprehension skills and early literacy skills.

3. Use the questions in the back of each book to guide your singing and storytelling.

4. Read the included sheet music with your child while you listen to the song. How do the music notes correlate to the words of the song?

5. Sing along on the go and at home. Access music by scanning the QR code on each Cantata book. You can also stream or download the music for free to your computer, smartphone, or mobile device.

Devoting time to daily reading shows that you are available for your child. Together, you are building language, literacy, and listening skills.

Have fun reading and singing!

In the United States, Thanksgiving is on the fourth Thursday of November. The **Pilgrims** began this holiday in celebration of their first harvest in the Americas. Today, we celebrate Thanksgiving with parades, family gatherings, and holiday **feasts**.

To learn what makes Thanksgiving such a special holiday, turn the page and sing along!

History gave us a special day.
Now we give thanks in many ways:
with pumpkin pies and stuffed turkey,
parades, friends, and our families.

Way back in the year 1621,
the Pilgrims at Plymouth were feeling glum.

Winter had been long, and they were hungry.
Oh, life was rough in the new colony.

MAYFLOWER

The American Indians sent Squanto
to help the Pilgrims get their crops to grow.

They were thankful for all the food to eat,
and the native peoples joined their feast.

History gave us a special day.
Now we give thanks in many ways:
with pumpkin pies and stuffed turkey,
parades, friends, and our families.

Back in the year 1789,
the **Constitution** had just been signed.

George Washington wanted to celebrate
by giving thanks on a special day.

History gave us a special day.

Now we give thanks in many ways:

with pumpkin pies and stuffed turkey,

parades, friends, and our families.

Way back in the year 1863,
Abe Lincoln served in the **presidency**.

He wanted to celebrate Thanksgiving Day.

He made it a **national** holiday.

History gave us a special day.
Now we give thanks in many ways:
with pumpkin pies and stuffed turkey,
parades, friends, and our families.

SONG LYRICS
Thanksgiving Day

History gave us a special day.
Now we give thanks in many ways:
with pumpkin pies and stuffed turkey,
parades, friends, and our families.

Way back in the year 1621,
the Pilgrims at Plymouth were feeling glum.
Winter had been long, and they were
    hungry.
Oh, life was rough in the new colony.

The American Indians sent Squanto
to help the Pilgrims get their crops to grow.
They were thankful for all the food to eat,
and the native peoples joined their feast.

History gave us a special day.
Now we give thanks in many ways:
with pumpkin pies and stuffed turkey,
parades, friends, and our families.

Back in the year 1789,
the Constitution had just been signed.
George Washington wanted to celebrate
by giving thanks on a special day.

History gave us a special day.
Now we give thanks in many ways:
with pumpkin pies and stuffed turkey,
parades, friends, and our families.

Way back in the year 1863,
Abe Lincoln served in the presidency.
He wanted to celebrate Thanksgiving Day.
He made it a national holiday.

History gave us a special day.
Now we give thanks in many ways:
with pumpkin pies and stuffed turkey,
parades, friends, and our families.

Thanksgiving Day

Americana
Erik Koskinen

Chorus

History gave us a special day. Now we give thanks in many ways: with pumpkin pies and stuffed turkey, pa-

rades, friends, and our families.

1, 2, 3. *Last Time*

Verse

1. Way back in the year sixteen-twenty-one, the Pilgrims at Plymouth were feeling glum.

Winter had been long, and they were hungry. Oh, life was rough in the new colony.

Verse 2
The American Indians sent Squanto
to help the Pilgrims get their crops to grow.
They were thankful for all the food to eat,
and the native peoples joined their feast.

Chorus

Verse 3
Back in the year 1789,
the Constitution had just been signed.
George Washington wanted to celebrate
by giving thanks on a special day.

Chorus

Verse 4
Way back in the year 1863,
Abe Lincoln served in the presidency.
He wanted to celebrate Thanksgiving Day.
He made it a national holiday.

Chorus

23

GLOSSARY

Constitution—the basic principles and laws by which the United States is governed

feast—a large meal for a holiday or special occasion

national—shared by the whole country

Pilgrims—the first group of people who left England to settle at Plymouth in 1620

presidency—the position of leader of the country

GUIDED READING ACTIVITIES

1. Put your hand on a sheet of paper and then trace around it with a crayon. Now use this to draw a turkey. Your thumb will be its head while your fingers are its feathers.

2. Do you have a feast at your house on Thanksgiving? What foods does your family make? Which ones are your favorite?

3. Have you ever watched a parade? Was it on Thanksgiving? If not, was it on some other holiday? What did you see during the parade?

TO LEARN MORE

Appleby, Alex. *Thanksgiving!* New York: Gareth Stevens, 2014.

Bullard, Lisa. *Grace's Thanksgiving*. Minneapolis: Millbrook Press, 2013.

Felix, Rebecca. *We Celebrate Thanksgiving in Fall*. Ann Arbor, MI: Cherry Lake, 2013.

Rissman, Rebecca. *Thanksgiving*. Chicago: Heinemann Library, 2011.